Fix that rocket!

Written by Teresa Heapy

Illustrated by Jon Stuart

Collins

Pam and Matt set off in a rocket.

They shoot high into orbit.

It feels a bit too hot.

4

Turn on the fan.

Now it feels a bit too cool.

9

11

Rocket

🐾 Review: After reading 🐾

Use your assessment from hearing the children read to choose any GPCs, words or tricky words that need additional practice.

Read 1: Decoding

- Reread page 9, and discuss the meaning of **sure**. Ask: Why is Matt asking Pam if she is sure (*certain*) that he should push the button? (e.g. *he's worried about what will happen*)
- Ask the children to find a word for each sound. Give them a page to read aloud for each, while the rest of the children listen for the sound.

  /or/ (page 3, *orbit*)   /ee/ (page 4, *feels*)   /ur/ (page 5, *turn*)   /ow/ (page 7, *Now*)

- Ask the children to blend the sounds in their head before they read these words.

  rocket   **orbit**   **button**   **better**   **loop**

Read 2: Prosody

- Ask children to take the part of Pam or Matt, and read their dialogue with expression on pages 8 and 9.
  - On page 8, discuss how Pam is feeling. (*she's very cold and desperate to get warm*)
  - Encourage the children to read Pam's words as if she wants Matt to be quick.
  - On page 9, discuss how Matt is feeling. (*nervous*)
  - Ask the children to read his words as if he is a bit scared.

Read 3: Comprehension

- Ask the children whether they have been too hot or two cold. What did they do to warm up/cool down?
- Discuss the title of the story. Ask:
  - What was wrong with the rocket first? (*it was too hot*)
  - How did Matt fix it? (*Matt turned on a fan*)
  - What was the second thing that was wrong with the rocket? (*it was too cool*)
  - How did they fix it? (*Matt pressed a button*)
  - How do we know they fixed the rocket? (*they do a high-five on page 10*)
- Challenge the children to retell the story using the pictures on pages 14 and 15. Encourage them to explain what Matt and Pam are saying, and what the rocket is doing.